BLENDED VOICES:
BLENDING THE VOICES OF VIRGINIA POETS

KATHLEEN P. DECKER
SOFIA M. STARNES
EDITORS

ISBN 978-1-962935-00-5

Published by High Tide Publications, Inc.
Deltaville, Virginia
www.hightidepublications.com

TABLE OF CONTENTS

FOREWORD

Good poetry anthologies are a joy to read and a treat for the literary inclined. Or for the lover of words. Or for those who value what brings creative minds together and the idiosyncrasies that make them distinct. Or… we could go on *ad infinitum*, because there is indeed much to love about a good poetry anthology. Of course, what makes an anthology good is, foremost, the quality of the poems in it. *Blended Voices: Blending the Voices of Past and Present Virginia Poets* is an offering of such poems.

When asked to submit to an anthology poets tend to send their best work. After all, those poems will epitomize their voice among other admirable voices, their one-of-a-kind wordplay in the company of other no less unique verbal repartees. So, it is not surprising that the poems you are about to read are very good poems. Not only that, they are also *intriguing* poems. Each of them incorporates history, a turn of phrase no longer used, an image through someone else's eyes. Most importantly, they resurrect the voice of a long-gone Virginian, who is nonetheless today's Virginian, and they give that voice a surprisingly fresh setting.

The historic poets whose works were selected for this literary venture are present in every poem of this book. Verses they wrote decades or over a century ago have found expressive homes among new verses, new syncopations, new accents. Diversity is a wondrous gift, which is why we celebrate it, but we could not understand or value diversity without recognizing what unites us. Things are different in one way, only because they are alike in a fundamental way. Change exists because our core identities do not. It is that unifying core—the human heart—that allows us to reach out, to hold on, in order to grow as one and as various creative beings. That same core makes it possible to assume what may seem a thing of the past into what is newly born.

Blending Voices is a small but, I think, vital contribution to this idea, this hope, for Virginia. The anthology celebrates the voices of our literary forbears, by exemplifying how they can be and are part of our voices. The collection also gathers the voices of today's Virginians, with our own diverse backgrounds, our own stories. We have a great deal to share, to lift up, to value in one another, while delving into and affirming what makes us one. Through poetry, whether we write it or read it, or both, we are well on our way to achieving this valuable connectedness. So, turn the page, read, enjoy!

Sofia M. Starnes
Virginia Poet Laureate, Emerita

INTRODUCTION

The anthology *Blended Voices: Blending the Voices of Virginia* began as a Poetry Society of Virginia (PSV) workshop I designed during the PSV Centennial year (2023). The Centennial theme was to celebrate the diverse voices of Virginia poets. I conceived of the idea of highlighting historic Virginia poets from diverse backgrounds, with the aim of blending their voices with those of diverse contemporary Virginia poets. The second goal was to educate participants about historic Virginia poets as they prepared to blend their voices with those of the historic poets.

We had a small, enthusiastic group of participants for the workshop I ran in Richmond, Virginia, on May 6th, 2023, during the PSV Centennial Festival. The format of the workshop was slightly different from that of this book. In the workshop, participants picked poetry lines at random from four color-coded bins, one for each historic Virginia poet. The lines had been excised from two different poems by each historic Virginia poet: Edgar Allan Poe, Ruby Altizer Roberts, Anne Spencer, and Karenne Wood. Together, these authors represent several of Virginia's demographics: Caucasian male (Poe), Caucasian female (Roberts), African-American female (Spencer), and Native-American (Monacan) female (Wood). The workshop participants then created their own poems, using the four lines they had randomly chosen from the work of these historic poets. I presented a second workshop via Zoom to another set of participants.

For the book, I decided to extend the challenge to all Poetry Society of Virginia members. Since the contributors would be working remotely, they were presented the same two poems from each of the four historic poets—a total of eight—and invited to choose one line from one poem by each poet. From these lines, or woven around these lines, they each created a novel poem, thus adding their voices to those of the historic poets. As the reader will find, the result is a joyful selection of widely different poetic contents and styles. Most of the historic poems are reprinted in the beginning of the book, so the reader can understand the original intent and experience the historic poets' voices before they are blended with voices from contemporary Virginia poets.

Sofia M. Starnes, Virginia Poet Laureate, Emerita, has been kind enough to add her editing expertise and keen poetic eye to the process of compiling the anthology. We hope you enjoy the resulting collection, and that the blending of voices it represents will foster a further blending of Virginia's diverse peoples and cultures.

Kathleen P. Decker
Past Vice President, Eastern Region, Poetry Society of Virginia

THE HISTORIC POETS

SONNET — TO SCIENCE[1]

EDGAR ALLAN POE

SCIENCE! true daughter of Old Time thou art!
   who alterest all things with thy peering eyes.
why preyest thou thus upon the poet's heart,
   vulture, whose wings are dull realities?
how should he love thee? or how deem thee wise,
   who wouldst not leave him in his wandering
to seek for treasure in the jewelled skies
   albeit he soared with an undaunted wing?
hast thou not dragged Diana from her car?
   and driven the hamadryad from the wood
to seek a shelter in some happier star?
   hast thou not torn the naiad from her flood,
the elfin from the green grass, and from me
   the summer dream beneath the tamarind tree?

---

1 "Sonnet — To Science" by Edgar Allan Poe in *Al Aaraaf, Tamerlane, and Minor Poems*

To F_____ [1]

Edgar Allan Poe

Beloved! amid the earnest woes
that crowd around my earthly path—
(drear path, alas! where grows
not even one lonely rose)—
my soul at least a solace hath
in dreams of thee, and therein knows
an Eden of bland repose.

and thus, thy memory is to me:
like some enchanted far-off isle
in some tumultuous sea—
some ocean throbbing far and free
with storms—but where meanwhile
serenest skies continually
just o'er that one bright island smile.

---

1 "To F _____" by Edgar Allan Poe in *Poems, Tales, Selected Essays*

Cocoon[1]

Ruby Altizer Roberts

sleep well small ballerina in the jade
and gold rimmed casket of your transient dream.
hammocked in brief sobriety of shade
are wraith and substance of recurring theme.
your hour will come to flutter on the leaf
like some bright pertinent star against the bole,
and prove the darker firmament of grief
no more than backdrop to your lively role.
what substance of faith would dare to storm
this thimbleful of summer threaded high
upon the bough? while deep within and warm,
life taps a constant challenge to decry
the greater impulse waiting to be worn
and whirl before milleniums of sun.

---

1 "Cocoon" by Ruby Altizer Roberts in *Command the Stars*

VIRGINIA[1]

RUBY ALTIZER ROBERTS

to me, you seem most blest of any state
holding the claim inviolate to another,
the valiant dream and deed are yours and fate
has crowned you with the glorious name of mother.
your hills are regal, rising queenly-clad
from emerald valleys fringes with yellow grain,
your rivers and your dunes are free and glad:
the ocean touches you with silver grain.

on many an alien shore your progeny
have fought for right, your name upon their breath,
remembering the lesson at your knee
that flamed in words of "liberty or death,"
pain is your birthright, but how often this—
a nation finds in you its genesis.

---

1 "Virginia" by Ruby Altizer Roberts in *Forever Is Too Long*

Confession Beneath Plum Trees[1]

Karenne Wood

the air; enflamed throat of August. dusk spreads
riotous membranes at field's edge, beneath the arbor.
as my vigil becomes heat, cicadas tune up-
am I surprised, nearing forty, by landscape intense
as my life still on fire-I want, I want, rasp of cicada.
this is the world, its darkening plain, white-fenced
as ribbon strips bind a gift awkward to hold—
in this scene, why introduce regret? Walking through
Georgetown summers ago, past a gate wrought
with a pattern of orderly vines, what if I'd taken
his hand, kissed or uttered a phrase? Who was
betrayed? In my palm, the hot plum colored like a bruise
could be any woman's heart. It tells the whole story.

---

1 "Confession Beneath Plum Trees" by Karenne Wood in *Markings on Earth*

SMOKE[1]

KARENNE WOOD

These August nights, we sat by your workbench
in the garage and chain-smoked cigarettes
smoke clenching upward, hovering, its stench
blown outside. We talked beside cords, fish nets
wiring, hinges, clamps and cracked pails.
On a wall behind us, you'd traced the outlines
of hammers and staple guns, around nails
where they were meant to hang. At times
you'd found tools gone, while working on a flower
bed or deck, lost in piled leaves, their shapes
empty like chalked figures after a crime. Hours
of talk hurt us both—should I leave, try to stay,
which furniture belonged to who—through all
this, those vestiges on the wall.

---

1 "Smoke" by Karenne Wood in *Markings on Earth*

"Requiem" by Anne Spencer first appeared in *Lyric*, Spring, 1931, and "Black Man O'Mine," written ca. 1930, was republished by Nina Salmon in *Anne Spencer: "Ah, How Poets Sing and Die"*, Warwick Publishing House, 2001. The reader is directed to enjoy the full text of "Black Man O'Mine," in that book. Due to the wishes expressed by Anne Spencer's estate, we are unable to reprint either poem here.

"Requiem" is not easy to find in books in print, but we encourage our readers to access it in its entirety by visiting the following website: https://www.best-poems.net/anne-spencer/requiem.html.

THE CONTEMPORARY POETS

An Ode to Virginia

Sunanda Bhadra Bhattacharyya

Your rolling hills and countryside,
that crowd around my earthly path—[1]
speak to me as I walk.

The Appalachian Mountains;
your age-old sentinel echoes
the tales of your past.

Jamestown and Williamsburg—
brimming with history and heritage;
Appomattox and Yorktown reminiscence
the historical siege operations of war.

In the depths of the Atlantic lies the truth;
its ages of treasure to hold and to view;[2]
the Spanish and the British invasion;
stories of slave trade and colonization;
etched on every grain of sand.

The burning desire within you paved the path
that flamed in words of "liberty or death,"[3]
making it a land of equal opportunity for all;
and proclaimed yourself as, "Virginia is for lovers."

Descendants of once enslaved African Americans
are now representatives of the state;
this is the world, its darkening plain, white-fenced[4]
skyline, rippling rivers, the ocean and the Blue Ridge—
your confidantes for centuries, have witnessed it all.

---

1 From To F _____" by Edgar Allan Poe in *Poems, Tales, Selected Essays*

2 From "Black Man O'Mine" by Anne Spencer in *Ah, How Poets Sing and Die*

3 From "Virginia" by Ruby Altizer Roberts in Forever Is Too Long

4 From "Confession Beneath Plum Trees" by Karenne Wood in *Markings on Earth*

LOST SPRING

SUNANDA BHADRA BHATTACHARYYA

With its infectious touch, the piedmont is rolling green;
the pristine beaches break its freezing silence;
the Blue Ridge Mountains are out of its hibernation,
where daffodils and dandelions are in full bloom.

Oh, I who did drink of spring's fragrant clay,[1]
know how mesmerizing is Virginia's scenic vistas!
But, now, Spring seems so different;
it is so strange and still.

No more do I feel any rapture; I stumble and fall as
life taps a constant challenge to decry[2]
like the unpredictable rough wind that blows away
the untimely pink and white cherry blossoms.

I feel I have been amputated since
my nest has been disheveled by that fateful hurricane.
Am I losing my sanity for I fly like a
vulture, whose wings are dull realities?[3]

I soar on the vernal winds with a broken heart. Why am I
betrayed? In my palm, the hot plum colored like a bruise[4]
objectifies my wound. I wander around
like a lonely loon in the land of lovers' paradise.

To hide my pain and strife;
to conceal that I'm broken and fragile
from the world of mere spectators;
my sagacious lips complement it with a smile.

---

1 From "Requiem" by Anne Spencer in *Lyric*

2 From "Cocoon" by Ruby Altizer Roberts in *Command the Stars*

3 From "Sonnet — To Science" by Edgar Allan Poe in *Al Aaraaf, Tamerlane, and Minor Poems*

4 From "Confession Beneath Plum Trees" by Karenne Wood in *Markings on Earth*

To Autumn

Sunanda Bhadra Bhattacharyya

Striving like embers before the curtain falls;
your indomitable spirit is a streak of hope;
the valiant dream and deed are yours and fate [1]
has made you an adornment of the Old Dominion.

The vibrant rows of red, yellow, and orange fall colors
reinvigorate the spirit of Virginia before the cruelest time;
as Nature paints her canvas with charismatic strokes,
that glow like a fiery picturesque landscape.

I sit and contemplate at the verge of my twilight hours;
as my life still on fire - I want, I want, rasp of cicada. [2]
I crave for the warmth of the sultry summer
as I sip the last drop of nectar oozing out of nostalgia.

The rustling leaves fall on the ground
like graceful grieving teardrops.
The pall of dry November leaves
shield the dormant seeds to sprout in March.

I hear farewell songs of migrating birds;
my heart bereft—I might rest then [3]
Why not bid adieu to the world
to seek a shelter in some happier star? [4]

---

1 From "Virginia" by Ruby Altizer Roberts in *Forever Is Too Long*

2 From "Confession Beneath Plum Trees" by Karenne Wood in *Markings on Earth*

3 From "Requiem" by Anne Spencer in *Lyric*

4 From "Sonnet — To Science" by Edgar Allan Poe in *Al Aaraaf, Tamerlane, and Minor Poems*

GRAY-HAIRED WOMAN

MADALIN BICKEL

Oh, grandmother dear, you
sit before me in your faded chair
as if waiting. Perhaps you are.
I choose to remember time before your
worn down body left me with only
memories.

The ghosts of former times weigh
upon my mind and heart. I smell your
perfectly fried chicken; I taste your
lemon pie. Can you understand, you
who preyest thou thus upon the poet's heart[1]
that I need more than these memories?

Remember all those days when we snapped
green beans and shucked sweet corn?
These August nights we sat by your workbench[2]
where I learned to make a quilt? That quilt!
I have it still with fine stiches where you
appliquéd my mother's life from scraps
of blankets used and long forgotten.

I know the time will come, when your
grey-threaded hair lies upon the satin
pillow of your last bed. I must face reality.
The grave restores what finds it best[3]
And prove the darker firmament of grief.[4]

But grief shall not control my numbered days,
for you have left your magic and your strength
to nurture in my heart.

---

[1] From "Sonnet – To Science" by Edgar Allen Poe in *Al Aaraaf, Tamerlane, and Minor Poems*

2 From "Smoke" by Karenne Wood in *Markings on the Earth*

3 From "Requiem" by Anne Spencer in *Lyric*

4 From "Cocoon" by Ruby Altizer Roberts in *Command the Stars*

My West Virginia

Madalin Bickel

O, West Virginia!
Like some enchanted far-off isle[1]
I stand in awe
of your majestic mountains.
I marvel at your delicacies:
dainty dogwood blossoms, oaks and
maples deep green in summer,
burning red and golden in October.

I love your stalwart people -
your coal dust-streaked miners, hearty
farmers, sons, and daughters, gentle
souls long passed, and that the beauty of
your rivers and your dunes are free and glad.[2]

Historic West Virginia.
I ache for your past - quaint country churches
to towering spires, covered bridges to
steel cabled suspension wonders, curvy
dusty roads to four-lane mountain marvels,
this, those vestiges on the wall.[3]

I am humbled by your presence,
entranced by your beauty,
am consumed by the earth instead,[4]
and comforted to call you home.

---

1 From "To F _____" by Edgar Allan Poe in *Poems, Tales, Selected Essays*
2 From "Virginia" by Ruby Altizer Roberts in *Forever Is Too Long*
3 From "Smoke" by Karenne Wood in *Markings on Earth*
4 From "Requiem" by Anne Spencer in *Lyric*

RAPPAHANNOCK RHAPSODY

MADALIN BICKEL

Rain formed crystal streams
flow down Blueridge Mountains
among spruce and pine, oaks and maples,
crags and eyrie homes where eagles soar
to seek for treasures in the jewelled skies.[1]

The Rappahannock winds its way east
through hillside nurtured vineyards and
from emerald valleys fringed with yellow grain[2]
to fresh waters that boast reeds, a marsh hibiscus
bed or deck, lost in piled leaves, their shapes[3]
outlined amid shadows of frogs and herons,
racoons, and muskrats, who watch and wait.

Soon wetlands emerge from lowlands where
the river welcomes a brackish marsh with
narrow leafed cattails, fiddler crabs, and proud
osprey posed to dive.

The slow-moving water meets the bay
then the briny sea and man's impact:
thin-shelled oysters, crabs with one claw,
invasive species who devour what is left.
The echo of its history and life reaches my ears. I
am consumed by the earth instead[4]
and all that man has wrought.
Save me.

---

1 From "Sonnet – to Silence" by Edgar Allen Poe in *Al Aaraaf, Tamerlane, and Minor Poems*

2 From "Virginia" by Ruby Altizer Roberts in *Forever Is Too Long*

3 From "Smoke" by Karenne Wood in *Markings on Earth*

4 From "Requiem" by Anne Spencer in *Lyric*

A SUMMER FIASCO

LAURA J. BOBROW

This, those vestiges on the wall[1]
of the cottage in the dunes,
all that remain of a summer affair.
There the splatter of a broken vase.

There the imprint of a tumid fist
raised in utter disillusion.
There the outline of the clock,
a silent witness.

The pregnant bush being deflowered
by the shifting sand,
it could not give what I give to you,[2]
not even one lonely rose.[3]

Goodbye, my love, and just remember this:
your hour will come to flutter on the leaf.[4]

---

1 From "Smoke" by Karenne Wood in *Markings on Earth*

2 Black Man O'Mine by Anne Spencer in *Ah, How Poets Sing and Die*

3 From "To F____ " by Edgar Allan Poe in *Poems, Tales, Selected Essays*

4 From "Cocoon" by Ruby Altizer Roberts in *Command the Stars*

The Sanctuary of Love

Laura J. Bobrow

The earth shakes in violent agitation.
Pandemonium ensues.
An excited noisy crowd presses forward,
shouting, hands raised in alarm.
Hammocked in brief sobriety of shade,[1]
The summer dream beneath the tamarind tree,[2]
we cling to each other,
heedless.

As I hush and caress you close to my heart,[3]
Fire erupts.
Animals flee in noisy confusion.
but over our sacrosanct cocoon.
the air enflamed throat of August dusk spreads[4]
peace.

---

1 From "Cocoon" by Ruby Altizer Roberts in *Command the Stars*
2 From "Sonnet –To Science" by Edgar Allan Poe in *Al Aaraaf, Tamerlane, and Minor Poems*
3 From "Black Man O'Mine" by Anne Spencer in *Ah, How Poets Sing and Die*
4 From "Confession Beneath the Plum Trees" by Karenne Wood in *Markings on Earth*

VENGEANCE

LAURA J. BOBROW

If the world were your lover[1]
how should he love thee or how deem thee wise?[2]
The mountains rise like fulsome breasts,
the ocean touches you with silver grain.[3]
He thrills you with the delicacy of bird song,
the majesty of symphonic waterfalls,
vibrant sunsets,
the wonder of starry nights.

But treat the world cruelly and his wrath
is beyond comprehension.
Floods and droughts, perversion and killings.
His angry breath is like
smoke clenching upward, hovering, its stench[4]
unbearable.

---

1 From "Black Man O'Mine" by Anne Spencer in *Ah, How Poets Sing and Die*

2 From "Sonnet –To Science" by Edgar Allan Poe in *Al Aaraaf, Tamerlane, and Minor Poems*

3 From "Virginia" by Ruby Altizer Roberts in *Forever Is Too Long*

4 From "Smoke" by Karenne Wood in *Markings on Earth*

HISTORIC POETRY SLAM

WES CARRINGTON

'Tis quite a ghostly gathering, all writers in the room,
whispering their verses amidst the gathering gloom.
Someone lights a candle, another—a cigarette,
then they put their heads together, a Virginia poet quartet.

Poe pulls rank as oldest and eloquently starts
why preyest thou thus upon the poet's heart,[1]
the audience softly grumbles that this sounds a bit rehearsed,
and maybe, just maybe, the ladies should've gone first.

Karenne Wood answers Edgar, taking up this category:
could be any woman's heart. It tells the whole story.[2]
History becomes hers, a more recent point of view,
a child of the 1960s, and Monacan too.

Anne Spencer then arises, choosing careful words to impart:
as I hush and caress you, close to my heart,[3]
let's tend to our gardens, in poetry as in life,
carefully planting, and avoiding the knife.

Finally Ruby Roberts stands up to remind us of the "why,"
life taps a constant challenge to decry[4]
from the doyenne of poet laureates, a benediction of sorts:
may we all come together, in poetry and the arts.

---

1 From "Sonnet — To Science" by Edgar Allan Poe in *Al Aaraaf, Tamerlane, and Minor Poems*

2 From "Confession Beneath Plum Trees" by Karenne Wood in *Markings on Earth*

3 From "Black Man O'Mine" by Anne Spencer in *Ah, How Poets Sing and Die*

4 From "Cocoon" by Ruby Altizer Roberts in *Command the Stars*

Living Without Loving

Joan Ellen Casey

There is not a picture that paints it as well,
nor a melody that seeps into soul more deeply
than a poet's words that ring so true:
"for living without your loving is only rue."[1]

"These August nights, we sat by your workbench"[2]
planning…
"to seek a shelter in some happier star"[3]
knowing…
"pain is your birthright, but how often this —"[4]
clue isn't clear until the price of living comes due.

Now, with a blanket covering my eyes,
I lie alone, awake in the dark and see
my search for love I must pursue
without your love I am so blue

So, for myself and other I must imbue:
to not love again would bring even more rue.

---

1 From "Black Man O'Mine" by Anne Spencer in *Ah, How Poets Sing and Die*

2 From "Smoke" by Karenne Wood in *Markings on Earth*

3 From "Sonnet — To Science" by Edgar Allan Poe in *Al Aaraaf, Tamerlane, and Minor Poems*

4 From "Virginia" by Ruby Altizer Roberts in *Forever Is Too Long*

LEARNED BREATH

TERRY COX-JOSEPH

There are those days
when the sun refuses
to enlighten us, that yellow dwarf
of nuclear fusion stubbornly stationed
behind unyielding banks of fluff high above
the Chesapeake, when life lies
empty like chalked figures after a crime. Hours[1]
pass in tedium, repetition. Will existential
loneliness prod us
to seek a shelter in some happier star?[2]
But then the poets speak,
brighten the galaxy with human spirit,
wisdom, and meaning
that creates sense from senseless tedium,
tawdry tickle of time stretched
across the Appalachian trail,
and we exhale learned
breath into air[3]
that fills our lungs with purpose, passion
painted silver and yellow, more radiant
than the universe of stars,
until our sun, satisfied (and possibly jealous),
returns, joining us to awaken, to ponder, to create
and whirl before millenniums of sun.[4]

---

1 From "Smoke" by Karenne Wood in *Markings on Earth*
2 From "Sonnet — To Science" by Edgar Allan Poe in *Al Aaraaf, Tamerlane, and Minor Poems*
3 From "Requiem" by Anne Spencer in *Lyric*
4 From "Cocoon" by Ruby Altizer Roberts in *Command the Stars*

Oh! Virginia

Kathleen P. Decker

Oh! Virginia,
your rivers and your dunes are free and glad:[1]
save in the dark hours of the August hurricane
then with your passing dark comes my darkest part,[2]
shall all be lost, and naught be saved? Then
SCIENCE! True daughter of Old Time thou art![3]
Use your modern wiles to preserve treasures
so generations can venerate
the history of this sacred place

where my later Apollo gave
his hand, kissed or uttered a phrase? Who was[4]
this challenger, who dared to rival
early loves, in this, my last and favorite home
with all its peoples, their diverse voices raised
to celebrate the blending of cultures and races

settling in her rolling hills, blowing dunes,
and cool mountains
mixing makes this place,
as the sea sculpts the coast
as winds of change whirl the past to future
where I spend my final days.

---

1 From "Virginia" by Ruby Altizer Roberts in *Forever Is Too Long*

2 From "Confession Beneath Plum Trees" by Karenne Wood in *Markings on Earth*

3 From "Sonnet — To Science" by Edgar Allan Poe in *Al Aaraaf, Tamerlane, and Minor Poems*

4 From "Black Man O'Mine" by Anne Spencer in *Ah, How Poets Sing and Die*

On Being Bought, from Africa to Virginia: Part One

for Phillis Wheatley

Latorial Faison

     Blood into river, [1]
Black & murdered in old Virginia.
     Answer to thy Southern plea, cross
some ocean throbbing far and free.[2]

     My raptured soul, thy history's shame,
This is the world, its darkening plain, white-fenced.[3]
     O great white hope's hypocrisy
That flamed in words of "liberty or death."[4]

---

1 From "Requiem" by Anne Spencer in *Lyric*

2 From "To F_____" by Edgar Allan Poe in *Poems, Tales, Selected Essays*

3 From "Confession Beneath Plum Trees" by Karenne Wood in *Markings on Earth*

4 From "Virginia" by Ruby Altizer Roberts in *Forever Is Too Long*

On Being Bought, From Africa to Virginia: Part Two

for Phillis Wheatley

Latorial Faison

Bought & sold,
  Black man o' mine.[1]
Where they were meant to hang, At times[2]
  if not refined.

Beyond the veil,
  How should he love thee? Or how deem thee wise,[3]
With scars & stripes,
  and prove the darker firmament of grief.[4]

---

1 From "Black Man O'Mine" by Anne Spencer in *Ah, How Poets Sing and Die*

2 From "Smoke" by Karenne Wood in *Markings on Earth*

3 From "Sonnet — To Science" by Edgar Allan Poe in *Al Aaraaf, Tamerlane, and Minor Poems*

4 From "Cocoon" by Ruby Altizer Roberts in *Command the Stars*

My Home is Still & No Longer Tidewater

Andy Fogle

Think ships gorged
with so much want

in some tumultuous sea—[1]

blood into river[2]
gut into grain

a nation finds in you its genesis[3]

and me too, born into, born

of, borne by
and bearing

the same map of bonds

vein into root
bone into trunk
sheets of silver sweat

in the late summer squall
hands all over

this, those vestiges on the wall.[4]

---

1 From To F _____" by Edgar Allan Poe in *Poems, Tales, Selected Essays*

2 From "Requiem" by Anne Spencer in *Lyric*

3 From "Virginia" by Ruby Altizer Roberts in *Forever Is Too Long*

4 From "Smoke" by Karenne Wood in *Markings on Earth*

OCEANFRONT AFTER ALL

ANDY FOGLE

It's not so much the years as the mileage,
said a complicated hero from childhood,

and he wasn't wrong. After all, who's so foolish
to seek a shelter in some happier star?[1]

Just stay where you are, kid. Let the braid
of this and that be itself. Youngblood, succumb.

After all the hours of mirrors, all the smoke,
all the desire to be emptied, each

molecule consumed a talisman, every
turn toward the image of self-alone

a fall, a split, a withering, and now you know:
this is the world, its darkening plain, white-fenced[2]

and shadow-lawned, slate-roofed and blood-dawned.
You weren't far off with that notion of how

the grave restores what finds its bed.[3]
You always loved the beach. You always will.

Of the few immoveable human facts, that's
a two-for. Somewhere before *one* and after *all,*

is a land where nothing counts, where
every spot is a threshold, where *back home*

doesn't exist, nor longing, nor disgust.
Sorry couldn't make it sooner. Just rest.

You won't be on this shore for long; even now,
the ocean touches you with silver grain.[4]

---

1 From "Sonnet — To Science" by Edgar Allan Poe in *Al Aaraaf, Tamerlane, and Minor Poems*

2 From "Confession Beneath Plum Trees" by Karenne Wood in *Markings on Earth*

3 From "Requiem" by Anne Spencer in *Lyric*

4 From "Virginia" by Ruby Altizer Roberts in *Forever Is Too Long*

THE STORM

ANDY FOGLE

It's the truth. You show me who I am,
at fourteen years old, in the halfway house

of adolescent development, but
then with your passing dark comes my darkest part[1]

and there is no way to return
the petal to the seed, linked though they are.

You bring to my bedroom, twelve miles inland,
some ocean throbbing far and free[2]

and I'm awake in charcoal night. Thundersound
can move walls, one sense affecting another,

as the stories my grandmother tells me
of my father as a child changed the man

I think he is now, and the one I will become.
There is an old woodpile in the backyard's

far corner, and it always seems damp with rot, things
which never see light from under crumbling stumps.

How much time do I spend there, even now?
The light that dazzles comes from the void

in which we dream, but we think we're still
asleep, our memories suddenly

empty like chalked figures after a crime. Hours[3]
have nothing on days, which have nothing on years,

which have nothing on moments, which root
and whirl before milleniums of sun.[4]

---

1 From "Black Man O'Mine" by Anne Spencer in *Ah, How Poets Sing and Die*

2 From "To F _____" by Edgar Allan Poe in *Poems, Tales, Selected Essays*

3 From "Smoke" by Karenne Wood in *Markings on Earth*

4 From "Cocoon" by Ruby Altizer Roberts in *Command the Stars*

How Farming is a Joy, or Not

Eric Forsbergh

Oh, I who wanted to own some earth,[1]
like Jefferson. He brimmed over
with an affluence of ideals, but
experience drained him just as fast.
Yes, it was I who yearned to quit
the asphalt maze,
I who made that naïve oath
that flamed in words of "liberty or death."[2]

My wife and I, we purchased you,
you precious parcel of land,
and we began to dig, to trowel,
to get the tractor figured out.
We bought odd implements
we had to learn the purpose of. Later,
after that storm swept across the evening sky
and flooded the barn's equipment room,
we cleaned up a sodden heap of
wiring, hinges, clamps and cracked pails.[3]
Then as a dawn from Homer, with her rosy fingers,
arose, the six cattle we just trucked in from Helios
bolted, trampling our neighbor's fence.
The next afternoon
I lost my wedding ring shoveling manure,
whereupon my wife precipitously claimed,
while plucking chickens,
that she's not from farming stock.
Oh, we sold you soon enough
and thus, thy memory is to me:[4]
my fields of dream.

---

1 "Requiem" by Anne Spencer in *Lyric*

2 "Virginia" by Ruby Altizer Roberts in *Forever Is Too Long*

3 "Smoke" by Karenne Wood in *Markings on Earth*

4 "To F _____" by Edgar Allan Poe in *Poems, Tales, Selected Essays*

If the World

Eric Forsbergh

If the world were your lover,[1]
she'd shirk. Look at the way
you deign to treat the seas,
the skies, the soils too.
I'd care for her the better, guardedly,
as I gather nature close, warming to my task, and
as my vigil becomes heat, cicadas tune up-[2]
animals begin to howl-
the birds squawk-
Listen. They call you out,
abuser as you are.

Her better lovers plant themselves
not by the week, the month,
the year, but by the era.
They glance far forward. They dance
and whirl before millenniums of sun.[3]

Our lives should mimic those
of diverse prairies and fields bending to the breeze,
of purifying rains carried in a bank of clouds,
of trees wild with new growth, or of
some ocean throbbing far and free.[4]

---

1 "Black Man O'Mine" by Anne Spencer in *Ah, How Poets Sing and Die*

2 "Confession Beneath Plum Trees" by Karenne Wood in *Markings on Earth*

3   "Cocoon" by Ruby Altizer Roberts in *Command the Stars*

4 "To F _____ " by Edgar Allan Poe in *Poems, Tales, Selected Essays*

A PARABLE OF DELIVERANCE

CHAPMAN HOOD FRAZIER

Pain is your birthright, but how often this[1]
may wash over you, water of my waters.

All your loving is just your needing what's true[2]
to be a heart's parable that's broken and

betrayed? In my palm, the hot plum colored like a bruise[3]
ripens to an ache. Is this what we've come to

fruit of my fruit? Your desires washing us towards
some ocean throbbing far and free.[4]

---

1 "Virginia" by Ruby Altizer Roberts in *Forever Is Too Long*

2 "Black Man O'Mine" by Anne Spencer in *Ah, How Poets Sing and Die*

3 "Confession Beneath Plum Trees" by Karenne Wood in *Markings on Earth*

4 "To F _____" by Edgar Allan Poe in *Poems, Tales, Selected Essays*

SLEEP WELL SMALL BALLERINA IN THE JADE[1]

CHAPMAN HOOD FRAZIER

When I drove you to school that final morning,
you laughed, said, "I love you" and waving goodbye
danced into the school beyond the white fence.

Only later did I hear the sirens and follow them
 to where I'd left you, a place swarming with police and I
not knowing how a moment could bleed to grief

watched from behind the yellow line hearing shots from
inside; my throat burning though
I could not speak. The light itself cracked

empty like chalked figures after a crime. Hours[2]
stretched each second
oh, I who so wanted to own some earth[3]

found myself
in some tumultuous sea[4]
boiling within me as I drowned.

---

1 From "Cocoon" by Ruby Altizer Roberts in *Command the Stars*

2 From "Smoke" by Karenne Wood in *Markings on Earth*

3 From "Requiem" by Anne Spencer in *Lyric*

4 From "To F _____" by Edgar Allan Poe in *Poems, Tales, Selected Essays*

BELOVED

SUE DAVIS GABBAY

Babe unborn, I await the summer day when,
Beloved! amid the earnest woes[1]
of the world and of daily living
you will arrive; no matter beds unmade,
clothes un-ironed, all duties ignored.
As my vigil becomes heat, cicadas tune up,[2]
preparing a welcome for our first-born.
As I hush and caress you, close to my heart[3]
where you yet lie unbirthed—it is time.
Patience woven with pain, we strive together
Unaware of the world's joys and agonies.
Many hours hence, or few
You will come to flutter on the leaf—[4]
the first leaf of our family tree.

1 From "To F _____" by Edgar Allan Poe in *Poems, Tales, Selected Essays*

2 From "Confession Beneath Plum Trees" by Karenne Wood in *Markings on Earth*

3 From "Black Man O'Mine" by Anne Spencer in *Ah, How Poets Sing and Die*

4 From "Cocoon" by Ruby Altizer Roberts in *Command the Stars*

GIFT OF THE DANCE

SUE DAVIS GABBAY

sleep well, small ballerina in the jade[1]
green tutu. Little did you know at age six
that this was to be your last dance. No one
expected gunshots. You were dancing
as a tree; you were felled. A scream cleft the air; it
could be any woman's heart. It tells the whole story[2]
of three little dancers, Annie, Jan and Mimi,
who dance no more on earth.
We hope their spirits will fly free
to seek a shelter in some happier star.[3]
We love and honor you, three little girls
Annie, Jan and Mimi
Just for you living, just for you giving[4]
your gift of the dance.

---

1 From "Cocoon" by Ruby Altizer Roberts in *Command the Stars*

2 From "Confession Beneath Plum Trees" by Karenne Wood in *Markings on Earth*

3 From "Sonnet — To Science" by Edgar Allan Poe in *Al Aaraaf, Tamerlane, and Minor Poems*

4 From "Black Man O'Mine" by Anne Spencer in *Ah, How Poets Sing and Die*

The Poet's Advice

Sue Davis Gabbay

oh, I, who so wanted to own some earth[1]
in which I could plant the words stored in my heart
to blossom into poems I dream of creating,
have been denied; earth has responded only
with a pattern of orderly vines, what if I'd taken[2]
the poet's advice, would there have appeared a bud
or even two, to flower forth in story or verse? For
In all my earthly acres there blooms
not even one lonely rose.[3]
The poet has said "You need not that carved
and gold rimmed casket of your transient dream.[4]
Write more, try harder. You have much to offer.
Cultivate your earth, think before you plant.
Nurture your work, prune with care.
Your stories and poems will bloom.
These, not the gilt casket, will fulfill you."

---

1 From "Requiem" by Anne Spencer in *Lyric*

2 From "Confession Beneath Plum Trees" by Karenne Wood in *Markings on Earth*

3 From To F _____" by Edgar Allan Poe in *Poems, Tales, Selected Essays*

4 From "Cocoon" by Ruby Altizer Roberts in *Command the Stars*

Behold the Creature Cry!

Regina YC Garcia

Behold! See the harkening, piercing
vulture, whose wings are dull realities[1]
but whose eyes are sharp & keen
as it circles, eyes, smells, zooms in on the
struggling, the weak, the waiting
& those who have set their minds
that the end must come, even if feeling
no victory has been won on this earth
Now glazed eyes seemingly still, stuck on heaven
or at least Silence, are no longer looking at
where they are meant to hang. At times[2]
wondering how they are gone from this realm is of no matter
That they are gone is the anticipated prize

After the carrion creature has had it way, others begin
picking and winding 'round corporal flesh in feast
and prove the darker firmament of grief[3]
for in Nature's mind exists nary rift nor lack of measure
Taking life over in concert, whether in dry land or sea, &
knowing earth does not reject but repeats
is peaceful understanding…is the joy of matter
Sky hosts, Orishas, Angels, bear the spirits up while
the grave restores what finds its bed[4]
repurposes as fungus or flower or rich earth or cooling water
Indeed, it serves as haven or nourishment
for those in the circle who are still able to live.

---

1 From "Sonnet — To Science" by Edgar Allan Poe in *Al Aaraaf, Tamerlane, and Minor Poems*

2 From "Smoke" by Karenne Wood in *Markings on Earth*

3 From "Cocoon" by Ruby Altizer Roberts in *Command the Stars*

4 From "Requiem" by Anne Spencer in *Lyric*

Why Must We...

Regina YC Garcia

Why must we live in a world
where the truth of our existence is destined to be erased or
caked over by the grime of fear and forgotten or remembered only as
this, those vestiges on the wall?[1]

Brown bodies/Black bodies/bodies loving bodies
longing love acknowledged/protected
voices old/new/ancestral...
whispering for the gods of their understanding are silenced
...and the monsters? They've pulled our stories
screaming from shelves and poured them like
blood into river[2]
leaving us without memory
rushing us into rapids of confusion
pulling us down into the watery beds
disjointed and tangled in weeds, digested in the bellies of bottom feeders

We, who have crossed borders of hope, fled fields of fear
are now reminded by modern day mongers and overseers that
pain is your birthright, but how often is this[3]
that we must invent new histories, new ways of loving ourselves
placing ourselves in the seats of value
afraid to tell our children that
the land for us is failing and falling and
your wings may not fly you away

Must we now venture beyond these badlands
before it is too late to find some new Heaven?
The dreams of this one and the ones before
have worn thin, and now must we travel
to seek a shelter on some happier star[4]

---

1 From "Smoke" by Karenne Wood in *Markings on Earth*

2 From "Requiem" by Anne Spencer in *Lyric*

3 From "Virginia" by Ruby Altizer Roberts in *Forever Is Too Long*

4 From "Sonnet — To Science" by Edgar Allan Poe in *Al Aaraaf, Tamerlane, and Minor Poems*

GLOAMING AT THE DOWNSTREAM

MARJORIE GOWDY

sun sets soon in this Algoma valley
land of the Tutelo, long forgot
drumming of the ancients, of a kingfisher
blood into river[1]
this particular mist paints our faces azure
longing, tendered
the elfin from the green grass, and from me[2]
impatient sprites, us both: what say you?
you rest in wild ivy, eyes grey with uncaring
hammocked in brief sobriety of shade[3]
echoed steps, heron's cry, ghost whistles
this is the world, its darkening plain, white-fenced[4]
but not here, no fences.
folded river rocks bend as you rush by
just run

---

1 From "Requiem" by Anne Spencer in *Lyric*
2 From "Sonnet — To Science" by Edgar Allan Poe in *Al Aaraaf, Tamerlane, and Minor Poems*
3 From "Cocoon" by Ruby Altizer Roberts in *Command the Stars*
4 From "Confession Beneath Plum Trees" by Karenne Wood in *Markings on Earth*

His Garden at Twilight

Lyman Grant

My chilled Viognier, pale sunshine, paler, as evening
turns drear, and we sit inside the gloaming green.
I savor its light florals in approaching night
and refuse the urge to offer a tentative hand.
You have your soiled nails and your whiskey, so
in this scene why introduce regret? Walking through[1]
this richness, this bounty, months of salads, casseroles,
pies, aromatic sauces, we could toast your good luck. Yes,
the valiant dream and deed are yours and fate[2]
has been generous to you. More than to me--
(Where is my garden,
                    not even one lonely rose)—[3]
the breeze fails to rid the garden of its hungers.
If you wish to toast, let's toast, and drink too much,
then with your passing dark comes my darkest part.[4]

---

1 From "Confession Beneath Plum Trees" by Karenne Wood in *Markings on Earth*

2 From "Virginia" by Ruby Altizer Roberts in *Forever Is Too Long*

3 From "To F _____" by Edgar Allan Poe in *Poems, Tales, Selected Essays*

4 From "Black Man O'Mine" by Anne Spencer in *Ah, How Poets Sing and Die*

WISHING

LYMAN GRANT

it is a fretful way to live, attuned
to passing clouds, watching horizons shift
in shades of gray—ash or carbon, charcoal or slate.
dry hope desiccates into despair.
you do not crave to court disaster, but
the air; inflamed throat of August. dust spreads,[1]
contaminant, virus, silicate plague. You pray
what substance of faith would dare to storm,[2]
to cool, to wet, to weigh a comfort upon the earth,
or wash, perhaps, cruelly, away your neighbors'
house and crops, their livelihood, their kin
just for you living, just for you giving[3]
in to another one of hell's seasons on your knees.
faith or faithlessness? both fill us
with storms—but where meanwhile[4]
we burn and ache for sweet salves of petrichor,
somewhere a thunderhead listens, darkening
the skies preparing for the deluge.

---

1 From "Confession Beneath Plum Trees" by Karenne Wood in *Markings on Earth*
2 From "Cocoon" by Ruby Altizer Roberts in *Command the Stars*
3 From "Black Man O'Mine" by Anne Spencer in *Ah, How Poets Sing and Die*
4 From "To F _____" by Edgar Allan Poe in *Poems, Tales, Selected Essays*

EVOLUTION

CLAY HARRISON

the grave restores what finds its bed.[1]
like a worm confined to its cocoon.
your hour will come to flutter on the leaf[2]
you shall gaze again upon sun and moon.
Day by day, a miracle's taking place
unseen by human eyes,
unobserved by children at their play
as the worm becomes a butterfly!

this is the world, its darkening plain, white-fenced[3]
façade forever evolving and renewing
to seek a shelter in some happier star?[4]
while on earth below, the seasons keep revolving.
The grave cannot retain us when we die—
we too shall rise up like a butterfly!

---

1 From "Requiem" by Anne Spencer in *Lyric*

2 From "Cocoon" by Ruby Altizer Roberts in *Command the Stars*

3 From "Confession Beneath Plum Trees" by Karenne Wood in *Markings on Earth*

4 From "Sonnet — To Science" by Edgar Allan Poe in *Al Aaraaf, Tamerlane, and Minor Poems*

THE CHALLENGE

CLAY HARRISON

life taps a constant challenge to decry [1]
man's constant inhumanity to man.
oh, I who did drink of spring's fragrant clay, [2]
must respond and challenge what I can.
Are we standing on the edge of time
all across the U.S.A.?
Is this our nation's dystopia
spreading doubts and fears our way?

why preyest thou upon the poet's heart, [3]
to speak truth to power, have my say,
smoke clenching upward, hovering, its stench [4]
lingering from the mass shooting today!
Is this the wild, wild west on steroids;
will we live to fight another day?

---

1 From "Cocoon" by Ruby Altizer Roberts in *Command the Stars*

2 From "Requiem" by Anne Spencer in *Lyric*

3 From "Sonnet – To Science" by Edgar Allan Poe in *Al Aaraaf, Tamerlane, and Minor Poems*

4 From "Smoke" by Karenne Wood in *Markings on Earth*

THE OLD DOMINION

CLAY HARRISON

to me, you seem most blest of any state[1]
your historic past still reigns supreme.
There was no lovelier state on earth
to create the "American Dream."
oh, I who so wanted to own some earth,[2]
retired and made the Old Dominion my home.
my soul at least a solace hath[3]
wherever I may choose to roam.
in this scene, why introduce regret? Walking through[4]
old cobbled streets where patriots trod
from Jamestown, Yorktown, and Williamsburg
forever blessed by a loving God!
Every day becomes a memory-
there's no other place I want to be!

---

1 From "Virginia" by Ruby Altizer Roberts in *Forever is Too Long*

2 From "Requiem" by Anne Spencer in *Lyric*

3 From "To F_____" by Edgar Allan Poe in *Poems, Tales, Selected Essays*

4 From "Confession Beneath Plum Trees" by Karenne Wood in *Markings on Earth*

PRESENCE

MAURA H. HARRISON

The unum necessarium—the smile
Of sense of Presence—multiplies
The sun and tunes the air of bee-laud skies
Like some enchanted far-off isle.[1]

This thimbleful of summer threaded high—[2]
Each flower's bower—sways delight
And marvels miracle, motion that might
Stir dobson, fire, and dragonfly.

Sweet industry of my beloved bee
Soon autumn-yawned with shortened hour.
You'd found tools gone, while working on a flower,[3]
And slowly ceased your carpentry.

December dried and cracked the pod-full dead,
Spilling a bit of ecstasy,
And burying seeds in snows of dormancy.
The grave restores what finds its bed.[4]

---

1 From "To F_____" by Edgar Allan Poe in *Poems, Tales, Selected Essays*

2 From "Cocoon" by Ruby Altizer Roberts in *Command the Stars*

3 From "Smoke" by Karenne Wood in *Markings on Earth*

4 From "Requiem" by Anne Spencer in *Lyric*

SOME OCEAN

MAURA H. HARRISON

I giggle like
Some ocean throbbing far and free.[1]
You bob your eyes
Like bottles, secrets in the sea.

I shiver like
Some ocean swirling riggings and a sail.
You're lost and stranded,
Wiring, hinges, clamps and crackèd pail.[2]

I'm breathless like
A stormy reckless wave, pounding and crashing
Breath into air,[3]
Surge into swell. My ocean spray is lashing

The tidal pool
with jellyfish and shells, baubles and glass,
a baby shark,
exploded fireworks, silky sea grass.

You're sitting like
A message—Save Our Souls! Your words contain
A moonlit song and
The ocean touches you with silver grain.[4]

---

1 From "To F _____" by Edgar Allan Poe in *Poems, Tales, Selected Essays*

2 From "Smoke" by Karenne Wood in *Markings on Earth*

3 From "Requiem" by Anne Spencer in *Lyric*

4 From "Virginia" by Ruby Altizer Roberts in *Forever Is Too Long*

THE HUMAN HEART

MAURA H. HARRISON

Four chambers sing with blood—
                                      heart's pulsed quartet—
Bold beckoning beats, infinity condensed.
This is the world, its darkening plain, white-fenced[1]
With ribs and set with soul, human vignette.
A trillion to the trillionth power made—
Unique and unrepeatable—we drum
The dark in different ways, a life-long hum,
Hammocked in brief sobriety of shade.[2]

Dark settings, pronged with toil and rhythmic drone,
What is a heart of Abraham's sky to do?
To seek a shelter in some happier star?[3]
No. Let the troubles tune your song and bone.
Shelter in Sacred Heart. Let death pursue!
Bone into land—[4]
                    We'll rise from where we are.

---

1 From "Confession Beneath Plum Trees" by Karenne Wood in *Markings on Earth*

2 From "Cocoon" by Ruby Altizer Roberts in *Command the Stars*

3 From "Sonnet — To Science" by Edgar Allan Poe in *Al Aaraaf, Tamerlane, and Minor Poems*

4 From "Requiem" by Anne Spencer in *Lyric*

This Night, My Dear

Jennifer Randall Hotz

We still look for them out here,
though they left home long ago:
the air; enflamed throat of August, dusk spreads[1]
fireflies flash lanterns of light,
pirouette around the yard
where our children once roamed.

Once we woke them up
in the middle of the night,
to seek for treasure in the jeweled skies[2]
spread out sleeping bags,
placed Thermoses of
hot chocolate nearby,
promised waffles for breakfast--
if only they'd stay awake to
watch the Leonid meteors
strafe the moonless sky.

Tonight, this yard—
its ages of treasure to hold and to view[3]
becomes something neither you nor I can bear:
life taps a constant challenge to decry[4]
the Norway maple
the single swing
the way the grassy spot
where they played pretend
never grew back again.

---

1 From "Confession Beneath Plum Trees" by Karenne Wood in *Markings on Earth*

2 From "Sonnet – To Science" by Edgar Allan Poe in *Al Aaraaf, Tamerlane, and Minor Poems*

3 From "Black Man O'Mine" by Anne Spencer *Ah, How Poets Sing and Die*

4 From "Cocoon" by Ruby Altizer Roberts in *Command the Stars*

Hot Dog Island

Mark Hudson

Like some enchanted far-off isle,[1]
Come have a hot dog and a smile.
Maybe even have some French fries,
This thimbleful of summer threaded high.[2]
A man at a counter stands alone,
his face familiar, his name unknown.
A lifetime career, "How do you do?"
In this scene, why introduce regret? Walking through[3]
Bring a friend to dine on fast food,
even though the cook is in a bad mood.
I would feel the same way too,
It could not give what I give to you.[4]
Where is this island, of which I speak?
Is it a far-off isle somewhere that is Greek?
It's Hot Dog Island, in Evanston, Illinois,
where there is great food to enjoy.
In the middle of the intersection it sits,
you can eat hot dogs bit by bit.
The only place left with pinball games,
since the seventies, it has been the same.
It's a little island, on cement,
which your stomach will feel like it went!

---

1 From "To F _____" by Edgar Allan Poe in *Poems, Tales, Selected Essays*

2 From "Cocoon" by Ruby Altizer Roberts in *Command the Stars*

3 From "Confession Beneath Plum Trees" by Karenne Wood in *Markings on Earth*

4 From "Black Man O'Mine" by Anne Spencer in *Ah, How Poets Sing and Die*

OVERDOSE

MARK HUDSON

Have you gone out to a celebrity bar?
To seek shelter in some happier star?[1]
My girlfriend seems to hate me again,
give back its wine to other men[2]
She lived deluded in her Jim Beam,
and gold rimmed casket of your transient dream[3]
My stomach started to get upset,
in the garage, and chain-smoked cigarettes.[4]

She was never meant to be,
not only just with me.
Like a flaming glimpse of the sun,
and then the cold darkness comes.
At the funeral, I didn't even cry,
but now I'm wondering why.
Another overdose, I couldn't foresee,
all I can say is I'm glad it's not me.

---

1 From "Sonnet — To Science" by Edgar Allan Poe in *Al Aaraaf, Tamerlane, and Minor Poems*
2 From "Requiem" by Anne Spencer in *Lyric*
3 From "Cocoon" by Ruby Altizer Roberts in *Command the Stars*
4 From "Smoke" by Karenne Wood in *Markings on Earth*

SUMMER DREAMS

MARK HUDSON

The same dream beneath the tamarind tree![1]
The hummingbird and the bumble bee!
Am I starting to feel a chill in the air?
Autumn coming, time to prepare!
Are wraith and substance of recurring theme?[2]
Do I have summer nightmares, or dreams?
Am I lounging my head on a pillow?
Should I be by the creek, and the willow?
Under a tree, a book is read.
The air, explained throat of August, dust spreads[3]
And in the morning, I find mourning,
But the blue sky I am adorning.
I better be more observant, instead,
The grave restores what it finds its bed.[4]
I lie in bed, lazy as a sluggard,
outdoors, I'd be a target for a buzzard.
The ant works harder than I do,
but then again, what else is new?
On the ground I see a caterpillar,
I nod off to my paperback thriller!
The internet says new jobs have been made,
and they're going to cut short government aid.
The government is always making threats,
to cover up their spending debts
Nonetheless, am I patriotic?
Hopefully I'm not psychotic.
A few bad cooks don't spoil the both,
I will just take another summer off.
My dreams may be your nightmares,
that all reality would disappear.

---

1 From "Sonnet — To Science" by Edgar Allan Poe in *Al Aaraaf, Tamerlane, and Minor Poems*

2 From "Cocoon" by Ruby Altizer Roberts in *Command the Stars*

3 From "Confession Beneath Plum Trees" by Karenne Wood in *Markings on Earth*

4 From "Requiem" by Anne Spencer in *Lyric*

AFTER LIFE, STARS

DONNA ISAAC

When it is time to leave this earth,
to seek a shelter in some happier star,[1]
there together we will whirl and spin
and look down upon our former earthly orb.
Let it be a final eternal light that we emit
over woods, the oceans, a place where
your rivers and your dunes are free and glad[2]
and where beloved kith and kin are content
or now mixed with dust, bone into land[3]
and soon around us shine in distant skies
where they were meant to hang. At times[4]
let us illuminate the night, inspire song,
and gladden hearts that sag with woe.
Beacons in the dark, we glow.

---

1 From "Sonnet – To Science" by Edgar Allan Poe in *Al Aaraaf, Tamerlane, and Minor Poems*

2 From "Virginia" by Ruby Altizer Roberts in *Forever Is Too Long*

3 From "Requiem" by Anne Spencer in *Lyric*

4 From "Smoke" by Karenne Wood in *Markings on Earth*

DRIFTING

DONNA ISAAC

A faint blue moon lights a sleeping child
who dreams she rises, then away she flies
to float through sifting clouds, beguiled,
to seek for treasure in the jewelled skies.[1]
With arms for wings, she rides breezes aloft
and soars above the rounded mountaintops.
Below, an exhalation of floating, misty white,
its ages of treasure to hold and to view;[2]
above, the hum of swans at greater height
like mother's lullaby the soothing sound;
ahead, a river wraps its arms around a field
so like a satin ribbon woven through her hair.
She dips and rolls o'er quiet towns below
the air; enflamed throat of August. Dusk spreads.[3]
All night the stars emerge, angelic guides,
until she tires and turns toward home again,
skirts the neighborhood, this fairy girl,
flits and flutters through willow branch unfurled,
wafts through her window curtained in brocade.
Sleep well small ballerina in the jade[4]
of evening shadows cast upon your bed.
Float down like a swan to reedy, peaceful lake,
find dreamless slumber, rest, until you wake.

---

1 From "Sonnet – To Science" by Edgar Allan Poe in *Al Aaraaf, Tamerlane, and Minor Poems*

2 From "Black Man O'Mine" by Anne Spencer in *Ah, How Poets Sing and Die*

3 From "Confession Beneath Plum Trees" by Karenne Wood *in Markings on Earth*

4 From "Cocoon" by Ruby Altizer Roberts in *Command the Stars*

UNDER THE AMFALULA TREE

—inspired by "The Dinkey Bird" by Maxfield Parrish

DONNA ISAAC

Oh, to be like the boy upon the swing
who soars and to the sky he sings!
He leans far back, stretched-out and strong,
breath into air,[1]
so filled with obvious joy
that those who see this playful boy
want what he has—freedom from constraints.
This is the world, its darkening plain, white-fenced.[2]
Some fearful things lie far below beneath the blue.
Here, he enjoys the fleecy touch of wind
upon his innocent face, permutation of mist,
a land peace-filled, calm, blessed, and kissed
by summer air, clouds of pristine white.
Your hour will come to flutter on the leaf,[3]
to reach a land
like some enchanted far-off isle.[4]

---

1 From "Requiem" by Anne Spencer in *Lyric*
2 From "Confession Beneath Plum Trees" by Karenne Wood in *Markings on Earth*
3 From "Cocoon" by Ruby Altizer Roberts in *Command the Stars*
4 From "To F_____" by Edgar Allan Poe *in Poems, Tales, Selected Essays*

WHAT AM I CHASING AFTER?

HOLLY KARAPETKOVA

what am I chasing after?
some ocean throbbing far and free[1]
as my life on fire—I want, I want, rasp of cicada[2]
whatever is out of reach
out past the breakers
the freedom of the current
to travel
and whirl before millenniums of sun[3]
to know no hunger,
blood into river[4]
river into sea
to touch every shore
the sands shifting beneath me
never still, slow to anger,
holding onto my secrets
miles deep
the indifference of salt
washing everything to silt

---

1 From "To F_____" By Edgar Allan Poe in *Poems, Tales, Selected Essays*
2 From "Confession Beneath Plum Trees" by Karenne Wood in *Markings on Earth*
3 From "Cocoon" by Ruby Altizer Roberts in *Command the Stars*
4 From "Requiem" by Anne Spencer in *Lyric*

VIRGINIA SUMMER

HOLLY KARAPETKOVA

Late June finds me once again
this thimbleful of summer threaded high[1]
the early sprouts of spring taking off,
filling my eyes with green:
in this scene, why introduce regret? Walking through[2]
the neighborhood heat rises from the asphalt
smoke from fires burning thousands of miles away
fills my lungs, settles in a thick haze
blurring the sunlight, the tops of trees
and still life is spilling over,
the way the planet keeps on giving
bone into land[3]
no matter how we've poisoned, ravaged
and driven the hamadryad from the wood:[4]
still this wild abundance.

---

1 From "Cocoon" by Ruby Altizer Roberts in *Command the Stars*

2 From "Confession Beneath Plum Trees" by Karenne Wood in *Markings on Earth*

3 From "Requiem" by Anne Spencer in *Lyric*

4 From "Sonnet—To Science" by Edgar Allan Poe in *Poems, Tales, Selected Essays*

WHY WAR?

EDWARD W. LULL

What leads us into war? Or do we seek it?
This is the world, its darkening plain, white-fenced[1]
at home, sleeping the sleep of peace.
Too often we fail to notice troubles, like
some ocean throbbing far and free[2]
with sudden fearful death to warriors and innocents.
Bombs and missiles turn landscape
Into craters, buildings into rubble and
blood into river.[3]
If dead could talk would they proclaim that you
have fought for right, your name upon their breath.[4]

---

1 From "Confession Beneath Plum Trees" by Karenne Wood in *Markings on Earth*

2 From "To F _____" by Edgar Allan Poe in *Poems, Tales, Selected Essays*

3 From "Requiem" by Anne Spencer in *Lyric*

4 From "Virginia" by Ruby Altizer Roberts in *Forever Is Too Long*

THE PRICE OF CHOICE

EDWARD W. LULL

Could there ever be a love like ours?
One with passion and permanence, blest by
serenest skies continually[1]
Sometimes, while walking, enjoying each other,
on a wall behind us, you'd trace the outlines[2]
of my favorite flowers. I loved it!

When your future seems bright and secure,
life taps a constant challenge to decry[3]
the best of plans. He chose a course
both knew she had no role.
Walking home past the wall
with his floral tracings, referring
to his choice, she whispered
"it could not give what I give to you."[4]

---

1 From "To F_____" by Edgar Allan Poe in *Poems, Tales, Selected Essays*

2 From "Smoke" by Karenne Wood in *Markings on Earth*

3 From "Cocoon" by Ruby Altizer Roberts in *Command the Stars*

4 From "Black Man O'Mine" by Anne Spencer in *Lyric*

CIÊNCIA

JOY MARTIN

You strain the calculus of my heart
to approximate the curvature of your arc
from Newton to Galileo to Einstein to me
and all creatures who herewith remain.

With nature-made you tinker, toy,
alter what you find scattered about.
You've manufactured a jumbled mess
with cause and effect pointing at each other.

With beaker, petri dish, spectrometer, heat, light
you transform convenience into plastic into illness
breath into air[1]
and prove the darker firmament of grief[2]

SCIENCE! true daughter of Old Time thou art![3]
Cracking molecules apart, you smile in the mirror—
smoke clenching upward, hovering, its stench—[4]
below, murky waters swirl.

---

1 From "Requiem" by Anne Spencer in *Lyric*
2 From "Cocoon" by Ruby Altizer Roberts in *Command the Stars*
3 From "Sonnet — To Science" by Edgar Allan Poe in *Al Aaraaf, Tamerlane, and Minor Poems*
4 From "Smoke" by Karenne Wood in *Markings on Earth*

OCEAN REFLECTIONS

JOY MARTIN

We traversed years upon solid ground
in separate searches of life's bounty,
ever-mindful not to lose footing. Then,

under a Venus Mars Conjunction sky
where hunter-gatherer selves align,
we left *terra firma* for Poseidon's realm.

As ribbon strips bind a gift awkward to hold—[1]
we suited up our disparate selves in star-crossed love,
allowing reason to surf to passion's shore.

Undulating waves crash rock, etch glass, polish shells
into sand-shadowed reflections on our incoming tide—
its ages of treasure to hold and to view;[2]

what substance of faith would dare to storm[3]
against such a bond that has no need
to seek a shelter in some happier star?[4]

---

1 From "Confession Beneath Plum Trees" by Karenne Wood in *Markings on Earth*

2 From "Black Man O'Mine" by Anne Spencer in *Ah, How Poets Sing and Die*

3 From "Cocoon" by Ruby Altizer Roberts in *Command the Stars*

4 From "Sonnet — To Science" by Edgar Allan Poe in *Al Aaraaf, Tamerlane, and Minor Poems*

Rooted

Joy Martin

the valiant dream and deed are yours and fate[1]
the soothsayer prophesied,
the grave restores what finds its bed.[2]

Young and full of pluck, I ventured out
to seek for treasure in the jewelled skies[3]
leaving comforts of home far behind.

Exotic climes, cultures, sumptuous cuisines,
momentarily savored, left me unfulfilled—
whether on pathways lush or barren.

One after another, seasons, people came and went.
Finally, I realized I was not meant to soar forever
but rather to sink roots in solid ground.

Now, beneath live oaks, I live my dream
surrounded by spouse, children, friends,
wiring, hinges, clamps and cracked pails.[4]

---

1 From "Virginia" by Ruby Altizer Roberts in *Forever Is Too Long*

2 From "Requiem" by Anne Spencer in *Lyric*

3 From "Sonnet — To Science" by Edgar Allan Poe in *Al Aaraaf, Tamerlane, and Minor Poems*

4 From "Smoke" by Karenne Wood, in *Markings on Earth*

SUMMER MORNING

SUSAN NOTAR

Arising early, in the solace of the still morning when
not even one lonely rose[1]
stirs, I search for respite from my sad reflections upon awakening
and hope, with the movement of the day, to dispel these ruminations.
Somehow simple actions:
making coffee, reading the newspaper, eating a muffin
help me mourn less.
On my back patio, the black-eyed Susan bobs, roses prick,
rabbits thoughtfully much on the lily leaves they can reach.
The heat has not yet begun to grip the air in a vise
this thimbleful of summer threaded high.[2]
Later, perhaps I'll walk to the farmer's market
relish the scents of fresh peaches and strawberries,
sample goat cheese and apples,
select bruised tomatoes and peppers, garlic, and onions,
to purée into a chilled soup.
In the evening we will grill and char meat,
how ancient the pleasure to sniff its scent.
We'll open a dark red wine and sip it,
and raising your glass you'll toast
give back wine for other men[3]
but we'll know we won't. It is just for us:
the air, enflamed throat of August. Dusk spreads.[4]

---

1 From "To F_____ by Edgar Allan Poe in *Poems, Tales, Selected Essays*

2 From "Cocoon" by Ruby Altizer Roberts in *Command the Stars*

3 From "Requiem" by Anne Spencer in *Lyric*

4 From "Confession Beneath Plum Trees" by Karenne Wood in *Markings on Earth*

CROWDED HOUSE

ELIZABETH NOWACK

I have not always lived in this valley,
an Eden of bland repose[1]
huddled in the broken
spine of the Blue Ridge.

      I was driven here by my mother's
disappointment, that crowded house
that could be any woman's heart. It tells the whole story.[2]
That never-ending tattoo:
all your loving is just your needing what's true;[3]
Pain is your birthright, but how often this[4]
leaves no room
to breathe,
to exhale,
to nick your fingers
on the pieces of your own life---

The valley here is wide like the plains
and the air is sweet with grass and manure.
With my arms stretched wide, I can touch
each wall, the door, the chipped windowsill.
All the echoes here are my own.

---

1 From "To F_____" by Edgar Allan Poe in *Poems, Tales, Selected Essays*
2 From "Confession Beneath Plum Trees" by Karenne Wood in *Markings on Earth*
3 From "Black Man O'Mine" by Anne Spencer in *Ah, How Poets Sing and Die*
4 From "Virginia" by Ruby Altizer Roberts in *Forever Is Too Long*

GRACE

PAUL EVANS SAVAS

if the world were your lover,[1]
stand tall then as a Tree -
whisper to cupid behind the shade,
shelter the swan gracing the lagoon,
and drink of the rain
with the worm and the rose!
the air; enflamed throat of August. dusk spreads[2]
to the night, to hide sweat drops of blood -
in the cool of the Garden (without the thorns)
the greater impulse waiting to be worn[3]
my soul at least a solace hath[4]
all is well with my lover,
Peace, all is well with my soul!

---

1 From "Black Man O'Mine" by Anne Spencer in *Ah, How Poets Sing and Die*

2 From "Confession Beneath Plum Trees" by Karenne Wood in *Markings on Earth*

3 From "Cocoon" by Ruby Altizer Roberts in *Command the Stars*

4 From "To F_____" by Edgar Allan Poe in *Poems, Tales, Selected Essays*

LOVERS

PAUL EVANS SAVAS

love begets love -
if the world were your lover,[1]
this agony would be joy!

the river winds itself away -
the greater impulse waiting to be worn[2]
by striving, love fades into the wind

wings without feathers -
the air; enflamed throat of August. dusk spreads[3]
hope has its hush, and love has its flight

love, to reach beyond our death,
my soul at least a solace hath[4]
which we all have, and thereby live!

---

1 From "Black Man O'Mine" by Anne Spencer in *Ah, How Poets Sing and Die*
2 From "Cocoon" by Ruby Altizer Roberts in *Command the Stars*
3 From "Confession Beneath Plum Trees" by Karenne Wood in *Markings on Earth*
4 From "To F_____" by Edgar Allan Poe in *Poems, Tales, Selected Essays*

PARIS

PAUL EVANS SAVAS

overlooking tree-lined Avenue Montaigne -
running from the Champs-Elysées
down to the River Seine,
my soul at least a solace hath[1]

if the world were your lover,[2]
the Plaza Athenée, and the Belle Époque
(and Christian Dior) welcome your soul,
the greater impulse waiting to be worn[3]

the air; enflamed throat of August. dusk spreads[4]
between the lampposts and the sky -
pour mon coeur!
bonjour and bonne nuit!

---

1 From "To F_____" by Edgar Allan Poe in *Poems, Tales, Selected Essays*

2 From "Black Man O'Mine" by Anne Spencer in *Ah, How Poets Sing and Die*

3 From "Cocoon" by Ruby Altizer Roberts in *Command the Stars*

4 From "Confession Beneath Plum Trees" by Karenne Wood in *Markings on Earth*

THIS IS THE WORLD

TERRY SHEPARD

This is the world, it's darkening, plain white-fenced[1]
garden of memories,
where you tried to convince me
that time was endless,
or the ocean would yield and you could discover[2]
something fabulous.

This is the world
where waves overpower us
and breathing becomes your focus, and
the ocean touches you with silver grain[3]
that slowly grinds at your mortality,
until you roll in the undertow
as current takes you away.

This is the world where
I crash to shore searching for that picket fence,
while griefs
that crowd around my earthly path[4]
hobble my footsteps home.

---

1 From "Confession Beneath Plum Trees" by Karenne Wood in *Markings on Earth*

2 From "Black Man O'Mine" by Anne Spencer in *Ah, How Poets Sing and Die*

3 From "Virginia" by Ruby Altizer Roberts in *Forever Is Too Long*

4 From "To F_____" by Edgar Allan Poe in *Poems, Tales, Selected Essays*

OCEANS APART

RODICA STAN

I grew up on the right river bank of the Danube,
Before it drifted into the Black Sea.

In summer time, from a tent on the sea shore
I dreamt for hours about the worlds beyond

Where the dark blue met the light blue. The regime
Did not allow regular citizens to carry passports.

I made up papers then and flew through darkness to see
some ocean throbbing far and free[1]

I pieced together beaches, waves, pelicans, and whales
Of which I read about in my Jules Verne books.

I hovered over ships and islands, when Ulysses whispered, "explore"
or the ocean would yield and you could discover[2]

At dusk, before a storm, I rolled with the gray chill, feeling how
the ocean touches you with silver grain.[3]

In an old port hunched under medieval history, I met a ghost
blown outside. We talked beside cords, fish nets[4]

And Poe poems about spirit, oceans, and freedom,
About how regimes come, go, rise, sink, kill, and die.

---

1 From "To F_____" by Edgar Allan Poe in *Poems, Tales, Selected Essays*

2 From "Black Man O'Mine" by Anne Spencer in *Ah, How Poets Sing and Die*

3 From "Virginia" by Ruby Altizer Roberts in *Forever Is Too Long*

4 From "Smoke" by Karenne Wood in *Markings on Earth*

PRAYER FOR FORGETTING

RODICA STAN

I wish to stop murdering you every day,
To stop seeing your guts and blood splattered
On my path to the garden where I sit in prayer,
I wish to wipe you off the present, off
the elfin from the green grass, and from me[1]

I wish for you to never die, to watch your child
Every day looking for you for one more tennis match
For one more trip into the mountains
For one more father-daughter ride in your Mustang -
my heart bereft—I might rest then[2]

I wish to have no recollection of your emptiness,
no more than backdrop to your lively role.[3]
And I wish to forget right now, at the end of this prayer,
Your "I do," your "I don't read any books," and you,
empty like chalked figures after a crime. Hours[4]
Of peace will rest on me, never hearing your call "amore."

---

1 From "Sonnet – To Science" by Edgar Allan Poe in *Al Aaraaf, Tamerlane, and Minor Poems*

2 From "Requiem" by Anne Spencer in *Lyric*

3 From "Cocoon" by Ruby Altizer Roberts in *Command the Stars*

4 From "Smoke" by Karenne Wood in *Markings on Earth*

Turn Off

Rodica Stan

You swipe left and right into a world of pixelated images,
A two-dimensional life of "pretty" enhanced by filters and mirrors

The persimmon tree in our yard carries your eyes from its branches up
to seek for treasure in the jewelled skies[1]

Your "device" bubbles up and spits bucket lists and "likes" and
Memes that laugh in a new cadence, with no lips, only teeth

We used to play hide-and-seek and train and read **Good Night Moon**, but now I
am consumed by the earth instead[2]

You click into a parallel world, your fragile soul drifts intoxicated, and I wish
your hour will come to flutter on the leaf[3]

Edited pics, emoji and sarcasm, you jump into the e-abyss,
Like the breeze always returning to the water's edge, I beg you to return
And we sit in the forest, in shards of light and solitude, empty handed, two
riotous membranes at field's edge, beneath the arbor.[4]

---

1 From "Sonnet – To Science" by Edgar Allan Poe in *Al Aaraaf, Tamerlane, and Minor Poems*

2 From "Requiem" by Anne Spencer in *Lyric*

3 From "Cocoon" by Ruby Altizer Roberts in *Command the Stars*

4 From "Confession Beneath Palm Trees" by Karenne Wood in *Markings on Earth*

Solace

Sofia M. Starnes

Late in the year, this, a familiar clip: a brew-
ing storm, a twig caught in a web at our window:
in this scene, why introduce regret? Walking through[1]
a door, I need not wonder how my hour, how

your hour will come to flutter on the leaf.[2]
Which matters most, you ask: the joy awaiting us
or the catalyst that takes us there? Oh, a belief
in the present, in being here, without making a fuss

about the partial story, the puzzle with a few
words missing; the page in a calendar, time-pressed,
its ages of treasure to hold and to view.[3]
I lean; the dip between your collarbones, a perfect nest.

Late in the year, this, too, a familiar scene, a path
that is, for us, root and resurgence. Blessed be!—
my soul, at least a solace hath—[4]
Remember how the backyard wept and bore a tree?

---

1 From "Confession Beneath Plum Trees" by Karenne Wood in *Markings on Earth*

2 From "Cocoon" by Ruby Altizer Roberts in *Command the Stars*

3 From "Black Man O'Mine" by Anne Spencer in *Ah, How Poets Sing and Die*

4 From "To F_____" by Edgar Allan Poe in *Poems, Tales, Selected Essays*

AND NOW. TODAY. LET US PRAY.

CAREN STUART

As dusk dayglows the threatening pickets,
>*this is the world, it's darkening plain, white-fenced[1]*
as protest riotous... riot, us... no. Know this:
>*then with your passing dark comes my darkest part,[2]*
Can you   see me?
>*vulture, whose wings are dull realities?[3]*
Prithee. See me. I am no bird of prey.
I am no bird of organized pray.
>*life taps a constant challenge to decry[4]*
I cry. Although...
Although.
This is surely
knot.

Enough.

---

1 From "Confession Beneath Plum Trees" by Karenne Wood in *Markings on Earth*

2 From "Black Man O'Mine" by Anne Spencer in *Ah, How Poets Sing and Die*

3 From "Sonnet – To Science" by Edgar Allan Poe in *Al Aaraaf, Tamerlane, and Minor Poems*

4 From "Cocoon" by Ruby Altizer Roberts in *Command the Stars*

PRESSING ON, LEANING INTO

CAREN STUART

Small but golden,
this thimbleful of summer threaded high,[1]
dawn's rising-up light is trickling down
as treacle tickling dew from the waxy, dark shields
of the sharp-tongued hollies illuminating
an uncertain, earthen path which is mine
to try to follow into the woods.
Here, as I choose,
in this scene, why introduce regret? Walking through,[2]
I will navigate where webs
have been woven into night, into shadow
then dew-kissed by morning's breaths
on the breeze to tease with faux glimmer
which dazzles as diamonds
then fades as gray bruises.
         bone into land[3]
I will go into wander. I will go
        to seek for treasure in the jewelled skies[4]
into wonder. I will press on. I will
press hope into heart. I will go.
        I will start.

---

1 From "Cocoon" by Ruby Altizer Roberts in *Command the Stars*
2 From "Confession Beneath Plum Trees" by Karenne Wood in *Markings on Earth*
3 From "Requiem" by Anne Spencer in *Lyric*
4 From "Sonnet – To Science" by Edgar Allan Poe in *Al Aaraaf, Tamerlane, and Minor Poems*

BOUNDLESS BEAUTY

DENISE WILCOX

O Shenandoah,
You spread before me
Your banquet table boundless in beauty.
Prussian-blue hazy ridges reach across
Serenest skies continually [1]
Pressing horizons to the west.
You saturate my senses with your glory.

Oh, I who so wanted to own some earth [2]
Claim you with my vision, my heart.
No deed of paper does this hand of mine hold.
I cling but to your mountain majesty.
Your hills are regal, rising queenly-clad. [3]
No youthful princess rising steeply in rugged peaks,
But rather, rounded, with age and dignity.
Am I surprised, nearing forty, by landscape intense? [4]
Nay, these mountains have cradled my soul
From toddler time to elder.

O Shenandoah,
From a distance, you beckon me westward.
My outstretched arms yearn for your expansive embrace.
Queen Mother enfold me, your child, too long gone.

---

1 From "To F_____" by Edgar Allan Poe in *Poems, Tales, Selected Essays*

2 From "Requiem" by Anne Spencer in *Lyric*

3 From "Virginia" by Ruby Altizer Roberts in *Forever Is Too Long*

4 From "Confession Beneath Plum Trees" by Karenne Wood in *Markings on Earth*

URGENT WHISPERS

DENISE WILCOX

The story is conceived.
Words
Written in the language of silence,
Settle and bury themselves in the womb
Until the message mirrors life.
This quietude, deep within,
Could be any woman's heart. It tells the whole story.[1]
Her story.
Of fierce love.
Radical hopes.
Outsized fears.
A world abundant with dreams.
Tender arms enfold the story and hum a lullaby
In urgent whispers designed to be carried
Through days, weeks, year-long verses.
At last, with open arms and a tight chest,
The song releases the story
To seek for treasure in the jewelled skies.[2]
Who will read this radiant story
And grasp her soul?
Who will understand
Its ages of treasure to hold and to view;[3]
And cherish each line carved from her flesh?
She lays it out like a quilt on a bed.
Myriad colors, shadows of dark and light.
A subtle pattern, patched and stitched,
Implores someone to wrap life's fabric around a naked body
For protection against a world too raw.
What substance of faith would dare to storm[4]
Her fragile essence and reveal the treasure of her story?

---

1 From "Confession Beneath Plum Trees" by Karenne Wood in *Markings on Earth*

2 From "Sonnet — To Science" by Edgar Allan Poe in *Al Aaraaf, Tamerlane, and Minor Poems*

3 From "Black Man O'Mine" by Anne Spencer in *Ah, How Poets Sing and Die*

4 From "Cocoon" by Ruby Altizer Roberts in *Command the Stars*

MINE

ELLEN WILLOW

Black man o'mine[1]
where have you gone?
pain is your birthright, but how often this[2]
rejecting to avoid persecution and
of talk hurt us both-should I leave, try to stay?[3]
So, we parted, each to our separate worlds
more bruised than e'er we met
and thus, thy memory is to me[4]
sweet joy and everlasting pain.

My heart flies with thee
as my wish for a kinder, more tolerant world
where we could love in peace
where beauty is stronger than color
and rainbows bless our union
where prejudice shrivels in the light.
Godspeed, God bless and keep thee
'til we meet in that happier clime!

---

1 From "Black Man O'Mine" by Anne Spencer in *Ah, How Poets Sing and Die*

2 From "Virginia" by Ruby Altizer Roberts in *Forever Is Too Long*

3 From "Smoke" by Karenne Wood in *Markings on Earth*

4 From To F _____" by Edgar Allan Poe in *Poems, Tales, Selected Essays*

Acknowledgments

"Sonnet — To Science" by Edgar Allan Poe, in *Al Aaraaf, Tamerlane, and Minor Poems,* Hatch and Dunning, 1829

To F _____ " by Edgar Allan Poe, in *Poems, Tales, Selected Essays,* The Book League of America, 1914

"Cocoon" by Ruby Altizer Roberts, in *Command the Stars,* The Wings Press, 1948

"Virginia" by Ruby Altizer Roberts, in *Forever Is Too Long,* The Wings Press, 1949

"Confession Beneath Plum Trees" and "Smoke" by Karenne Wood, in *Markings on Earth,* reprinted by permission of the University of Arizona Press. Both are from *Markings on Earth* by Karenne Wood © 2001 Karenne Wood.

POETS' BIOS AND STATEMENTS:

Sunanda Bhadra Bhattacharyya lives in Charlottesville, Virginia. She is a post-graduate in English Literature and completed the course *Masterpieces of World Literature* from Harvard University. She also participated in *Sharpened Visions: A Poetry Workshop* from California Institute of the Arts. She spends her free time reading, writing, gardening, hiking and travelling.
Statement: "Writing poems for this anthology was fun, exciting as well as challenging as we had to weave the lines of our great historic poets carefully and smoothly with ours. It was like putting a puzzle together. I enjoyed every bit of this journey."

Madalin Bickel, originally from Huntington, West Virginia, is an award-winning poet and author of cozy mysteries. Her poems have been published in numerous anthologies including *Scratching Against the Fabric* published from the first Bridgewater International Poetry Festival. She moved to Virginia in 2003 to teach middle school gifted students.
Statement: "Blended Voices, an anthology of poetry from past and present Virginia poets, was planned by Virginia poet Kathleen Decker. Kathleen held a series of workshops in which poets combined lines from past Virginia poets with their own 'new' creations. As a participant, I was inspired to delve into my own love of poetry to create several new and refreshing poems. I plan to continue writing poetry inspired by other poets and artists."

Laura J. Bobrow's poems have appeared in various media as far away as Abu Dhabi. A renaissance woman, she has been magazine editor, folksinger, song lyricist, sculptor, and painter. Her short stories have appeared in numerous anthologies. She is, in addition, and perhaps foremost, an acclaimed professional storyteller. Her website is www.laurajbobrow.com.
Statement: "This was my cup of tea! I delight in playing with the infinite combination of words to extract new ramifications. No philosopher I, but a born and bred game player. What fun and what a challenge!"

Wes Carrington is a former diplomat, now back in Fairfax rekindling his love of poetry through classes, workshops, and lots of reading and writing. While Wes has no poetry forthcoming, he does have a loving spouse, three great kids, and two cats who will not stay off the table.
Statement: "I learned a lot about these four Virginia poets in this challenging but fun exercise. I researched each author then highlighted the lines that inspired me in their two allotted poems, ending up with great material but no overarching theme. That's when, inspired by the music of John Prine ("Caravan of Fools") and the poetry of Ernest Lawrence Thayer ("Casey at the Bat"), I decided on a rhyming narrative, and the Slam was on!"

Joan Ellen Casey has written poetry since she was twelve, but never went public until 2011. Since then, she has won awards and her work has appeared in sixteen anthologies. Her writing is influenced by her life's roles, an insatiable curiosity, a doctorate degree, and trekking through twenty-three countries. She writes to share her experiences.

Statement: *"After having lost someone that I loved as no other, I found that Spencer's words took me back to that grief and guilt, when it seemed nothing was left. Then, holding my child for the first time, I discovered that loving was the most important thing to me. Today, I realize the love I lost has helped me seek and appreciate the many different loves I have found, which grew out of my need to love again."*

Terry Cox-Joseph is a past President of the Poetry Society of Virginia and a former newspaper reporter and editor. From 1994-2004 she was coordinator for the annual Christopher Newport University Writers' Conference and Contest. An award-winning poet, she has been published in *Northern Virginia Review, Allegro, Wingless Dreamer, and Chiron Review* among others. She displays and sells her paintings at On The Hill Gallery in Yorktown, and The Virginia Beach Art Center.

Statement: *"I decided to go with the commonality of the sun and stars from the works of Poe, Roberts, and Spencer then threading in Wood's unusual line, "empty like chalked figures" to dramatize days of tedium and even existentialism. I am pleased that I was able to include poetry as a form of creation that pulled in the elemental, original form of creation. Weaving in Roberts' dangling article and situating Wood's noun were particularly challenging."*

Kathleen P. Decker's Japanese poetry books include three chapbooks of haiku and *Whispers on Paper*. Her western-style poetry books include *Updraft*, and *Fishmas*. She edited an international haiku journal, *Chiyo's Corner*, and was an editor for the World Haiku Association. Among the anthologies she has edited are *My Neighbor's Life, On Crimson Wings, Quilted Poems*, and *Views of Virginia*, in addition to *Blended Voices*. She is a past Vice President of The Poetry Society of Virginia

Statement: *"I designed this project to challenge modern poets to read historic Virginia poets, and then blend their words with ours to create an entirely new poem. Use of archaic language blended with current language was a challenge, but emotions are timeless. I am delighted with the results everyone produced. My poem reflects my love for Virginia and science."*

Latorial Faison is a military spouse, mother, and native of Southampton County. She is a graduate of UVA, VA Tech, and Virginia State University where she is Assistant Professor of English. Faison is the author of *Mother to Son, 28 Days of Poetry Celebrating Black History, Nursery Rhymes in Black*, and other books.

Statement: *"I simply could not navigate these poems without thinking of—without paying homage to Phillis Wheatley. On these historic poets, their lives, and Virginia's storied chapter in American history was where my thoughts lingered. They lived, created, traversed their own Virginia, their own America, yet they culminates in an intriguingly kindred poetic spirit. I was challenged by their work, yet completely honored by the challenge of working creatively alongside them, with them, and through them."*

Andy Fogle is the author of *Mother Countries, Across from Now,* and seven chapbooks of poetry, including *Arc & Seam: Poems of Farouk Goweda,* co-translated with Walid Abdallah. He is from Virginia Beach, spent years in the DC area, and now lives with his family in upstate New York, teaching high school. He is poetry editor at *Salvation South.*
Statement: *"I blatantly avoided archaic language and predictably went with lines that had bodies of water (I grew up in Virginia Beach, with water everywhere) or landscape in some other way. I'm also a sucker for images that refer to darkness, mention fragments or traces or outlines and the like, or have to do with sources. From there, I just went with a few of my obsessions: home, history, the shore. My work can be found at foglejunk.squarespace.com."*

Eric Forsbergh's poetry has appeared in *JAMA, Artemis, Streetlight, The Journal of Neurology,* and multiple other venues. He has twice won the Poe Memorial Prize. His second full-length book of poetry, *This Mortal Coil,* appearing in Fall 2023, is about DNA and family.
Statement: *"In Blended Voices, I was drawn to vivid lines from Virginia poets as hooks for new themes, beyond the original line's intent. This project was fun as well."*

Chapman Hood Frazier's book, *The Lost Books of the Bestiary,* a finalist for the Virginia Press Poetry Award, contains work published in *The Virginia Quarterly, Southern Poetry Review,* and *South Carolina Poetry Review,* and been nominated for Pushcart Prizes. He has taught at JMU, Longwood University, SVCC and Murray High School and lives in Rice, VA.

Sue Davis Gabbay: A Virginian by birth, Sue Davis Gabbay is a graduate of Indiana University and of Syracuse University's library school. After a library career she settled in Virginia. There she reads, explores thrift stores, and builds poems with words old and new. Sue has self-published three books of poetry and several chapbooks.
Statement: *"Integrating other writers' lines into a composition was a way to create a narrative and, by doing so, to shift perspectives in terms of content and structure. Finding some way to blend the lines smoothly was most challenging. It is a matter of weaving each thread-like line to see what larger image or portrait emerged. The bigger picture was distinctly different from each source poem. This is the heart of the discovery process and what I love about poetry."*

Regina YC Garcia is an award-winning poet. Her work appears in various journals, reviews, and anthologies and is featured in an Emmy-Award winning episode of Muse (UNCTV), as well as the Tulane University Sacred Nine Project. Her book, *The Firetalker's Daughter* (Finishing Line Press) was released in March 2023.

Statement: *"In regards to my process for writing my collage poems, when I was finally able to wrap my mind around the rules for creation, I looked for lines that resonated with me. That made it easier to determine which direction I wanted to go. The easier it was to find a line that stirred thought the easier it was to create context in which the chosen line made sense. Sound rhythm and flow are important."*

Marjorie Gowdy writes and paints in the Blue Ridge Mountains. A Roanoke native who has lived throughout the Commonwealth and the south, Gowdy has three chapbooks, *Inflorescence: The Pasture at Rest, Cowgirl by Choice*, and *Horse Latitudes*. Marjorie was newsletter editor for The Poetry Society of Virginia 2021-2023.

Statement: *"It is daunting to include the evocative words of our best poets in my own rambling thoughts. Last spring, I spotted a Cooper's hawk at dusk resting on a sequestered tree limb. Her hiding led me to create "Gloaming at the Downstream" in concert with these famed poets.* **Hammocked**, *was she actually a* **sprite**, *or had she just tossed prey as* **blood into river***? For her, and me, the world can be a* **darkening plain***."*

Lyman Grant is an expat Texan living in the Shenandoah Valley. Once a college teacher and administrator, he now enjoys gardening, woodworking, and reading. His most recent book of poems is *ostraca* (4doorloungebooks, 2023).

Statement: *"I very much enjoyed the challenge of blending poetical voices from the past with my own, but I'm somewhat shocked by the overwrought dread that it produced."*

Clay Harrison's high school English teacher turned him on to poetry. He graduated with honors from high school and enlisted in the Army where he served as an MP, followed by 32 years as a Tampa police officer. For 60 years he has written poems of hope and inspiration, and he was a poet-in-the-schools for 25 years in Florida.

Statement: *"I absorbed the historic work of master poets. Combining my poetry with theirs was an honor."*

Maura H. Harrison is a writer, photographer, and fiber artist from Fredericksburg, VA. She has had works published in *Dappled Things, Ekstasis Magazine, Solum Journal, Amethyst Review*, and others.
Statement: *"On my first several reads of the source poems, I made a list of lines from each poet that either spoke to my imagination or to my ear. I then considered how grouping certain lines together suggested the boundary of a new poetic conversation. The process was a creative puzzle and I enjoyed turning the lines around until they fell into a larger poem."*

Jennifer Randall Hotz, a poet perpetually delighted by words, rhythm, and music, received an M.A. in English from San José State University. Her work has appeared in *Burningword Literary Journal, Naugatuck River Review, Connecticut River Review*, and is forthcoming in *Literary Mama*, among other publications. She lives in coastal Virginia.
Statement: *"Initially, I wasn't sure I'd like writing within set parameters and I felt intimidated by the poets who'd come before, sincerely hoping I could honor their words with my new creation. I started out by highlighting my favorite verses--once I'd done that, I could see the vague outline of a theme emerging and I followed that vision until this poem was born."*

Mark Hudson is a member of many state poetry societies, including Virginia. he found this exercise challenging, and he is a big fan of Edgar Allen Poe, and believes at one point he read all that Poe wrote. He enjoyed reading about other poets as well. To read more of Mark Hudson's poetry, go to illinoispoets.org.

Donna Isaac is a teacher/organizer of community readings/workshops and earned these degrees: B.A., James Madison University; M.A., University of Minnesota; M.F.A., Hamline University. She's published *Footfalls* (Pocahontas Press); *Tommy* (Red Dragonfly Press); *Holy Comforter* (Red Bird Chapbooks); *Persistence of Vision* (Finishing Line Press). A new collection, *In the Tilling* (FLP*)*, is forthcoming.
Statement: *"I loved the challenge of blending my words with gorgeous, rich lines from the four poets. I focused on lines related to nature and to the fantastical and played with these, juggling and experimenting, then creating my own poems with these integrations. I was also inspired by a Maxfield Parrish print "The Dinkey Bird" and connected with sky imagery and other images of the natural world from the Va. poets, which fit my sensibilities."*

Holly Karapetkova is a Poet Laureate Emerita of Arlington, Virginia, and a recipient of a 2022 Academy of American Poets Laureate Fellowship. She is the author of two award-winning books of poetry, *Towline* and *Words We Might One Day Say.*

Edward W. Lull published seven books of his poetry, including a historical novel, a memoir, and a text, a "how-to" book on writing form poetry. He earned a B.S. from USNA and an M.S. from GWU. He served four terms as president of The Poetry Society of Virginia. He was Editor-in-Chief of the *Poetry Society of Virginia Centennial Anthology.*
Statement: *"After reading all eight poems and not finding a natural linkage, I reread the poems carefully, to find a couple of lines I liked. Mentally, I began linking the two to form a theme for a poem. Going back to the unused poems, I picked a couple of lines that I could twist to contribute to the theme by adding words and thoughts to link the selected lines."*

Joy Mar was born in the South and resides in the Boston area and is a member of the Newton Poetry Group, The Poetry Society of Virginia, and New England Poetry Club and its board. Appearing in various publications, her poetry explores multitudinous facets of life, including her and broader humanity's place and challenges within it.
Statement: *"From the eight poems provided, I first selected all lines that resonated, then experimented with one line from each to write Dear Camille, to celebrate my granddaughter. Once I began to write within the specified rules, each 4-line set was allowed to determine its own direction. As poems emerged and edited, if needed I would revisit the parent-poems pool for better-fitting lines, allowing my message, my voice to blend and jostle with their historical ones."*

Susan Notar is a Pushcart prize nominated poet who has flown over Iraq in helicopters wearing body armor. Her work has appeared in numerous publications including *Artemis, The Bridgeville Review, Burningword, Burgeon, Gyroscope, Joys of the Table, Penumbra, The Poet,* and *Written in Arlington.* She works at the U.S. State Department helping vulnerable communities in the Middle East.
Statement: *"I enjoyed participating in this project because I found it challenging to try to seamlessly blend poetic voices from such different eras, and I also learned about poets from Virginia whose work I was less familiar with. Thank you!"*

Paul Evans Savas is an artist, poet, orthopedic spine surgeon, and lifetime member of the Poetry Society of Virginia.
Statement: *"The vitality of the book **Blended Voices** comes from the opportunity of the modern poet to collaborate with the historical poet in a novel muse. Through review of their works, comes the discovery of how each poet continues to speak to us today. By blending voices, in an indirect communion, their impressions continue through re-created impressions and interpretations."*

Rodica Stan is an emerging poet based in Alexandria, VA. She has contributed to a poetry collection, *Doctor Poets & Other Healers: COVID in Their Own Words* (Golden Foothill Press; Pasadena, CA), and to the upcoming issue of GRIFFEL magazine. When she isn't writing, Rodica works as a scientist.

Sofia M. Starnes is a writer of Philippine-Spanish heritage who has been an American citizen since 1989; she served as Virginia Poet Laureate from 2012 to 2014. Her chapbook, *The Soul's Landscape* (Aldrich, January 2002), was selected by then U.S. Poet Laureate Billy Collins as one of two co-winners of the 2001 Aldrich Poetry Prize. She has written four other books of poetry and edited two anthologies prior to *Blended Voices*.
Statement: *"The challenge of blending voices is its demand that we welcome, openly, other voices into what we often think of as a solitary, individual task. And in doing so, especially if we ponder the process a bit, we realize that, as it turns out, implicitly or explicitly, nothing we write is ever entirely our own. Even in our other poems, we listen, we echo, we borrow, we recreate. We are never alone. Let us be grateful for that."*

Caren Stuart is an award-winning, life-long intuitive poet/writer/artist/ maker living with her very supportive husband in the wilds of Chatham County, NC, where she writes daily, creates Convoluted Notions art and craft, and frequently hosts, helps with, and attends all manner of artsy/ writerly goings-on.
Statement: *"For my collage poems, I read the "prompt poems" once. Several weeks later, I scanned them for phrases that spoke to me, then wrote down the lines that contained those phrases. Once those lines were quarantined away from their poems, I began free writing "around" them. I like that the pulled lines ended up working like provocative interior dialogues which were running somewhat contrary to what the speaker of the poem may have been intending."*

Denise Wilcox lives in Keswick, VA. Family is her joy and nature is her peace, whether hiking National Park trails or watching her pollinator gardens thrive. She is an award-winning author who writes poetry and nonfiction for all ages. Her work has been published in *Paterson Literary Review, Ladybug, FunforKidz, Quilted Poems,* the Society for Children's Book Writers and Illustrators journal *Highlighter,* and *Developmental Medicine and Child Neurology Journal.*

Ellen Willow is a pseudonym for a Caucasian female PSV member.
Statement: *"The world needs to work a lot harder to accept or even foster interracial relationships. It was bittersweet to take Anne Spencer's happy love poem about her marriage, and blend it with my experience."*